ALL DAY SATURDAY

Charles Causley is one of our most distinguished living poets. His *Jack the Treacle Eater* won the Kurt Maschler Award, and *Early in the Morning* the Signal Poetry Award. He has been given the Queen's Gold Medal for Poetry, and the CBE for his services to poetry. He is a Fellow of the Royal Society of Literature.

After serving in the Royal Navy, he returned as a school teacher to his native Cornwall, to Launceston, where he still lives. Throughout his poems there are strong links with the Cornish people and folklore; both are continuing sources of inspiration. The poems in *All Day Saturday* range from the reflective Leonardo, who buys the caged wild birds in order to set them free, to the hilarious Knocketty Ned

> Who wore his cat
> On top of his head!

ALL DAY SATURDAY

AND OTHER POEMS

Charles Causley

Illustrated by Anthony Lewis

M

PAN MACMILLAN

CHILDREN'S BOOKS

First published 1994 by Pan Macmillan Children's Books

a division of Pan Macmillan Publishers Limited
Cavaye Place London SW10 9PG
and Basingstoke

Associated companies throughout the world

ISBN 0 333 60486 5

1 3 5 7 9 8 6 4 2

A CIP catalogue record for this book is available from
the British Library

Phototypeset by Intype, London
Printed by Mackays of Chatham PLC, Chatham, Kent

To Margaret and Reg Huzzey

ACKNOWLEDGMENTS

'Here we go round the Round House', under the title 'Singing Game', appeared in Charles Causley's *Secret Destinations* (Macmillan, 1986). 'All Day Saturday', under the title 'Days', first appeared in *Round About Six* (Frances Lincoln, 1992).

'Dawn at Ballintoy' was broadcast originally in the BBC TV Series *Play School*.

Contents

ALL DAY SATURDAY

Let it sleet on Sunday,
Monday let it snow,
Let the mist on Tuesday
From the salt-sea flow.
Let it hail on Wednesday,
Thursday let it rain,
Let the wind on Friday
Blow a hurricane,
But Saturday, Saturday
Break fair and fine
And all day Saturday
Let the sun shine.

I HAD A LITTLE CAT

I had a little cat called Tim Tom Tay,
I took him to town on market day,
I combed his whiskers, I brushed his tail,
I wrote on a label, 'Cat for Sale.
Knows how to deal with rats and mice.
Two pounds fifty. Bargain price.'

But when the people came to buy
I saw such a look in Tim Tom's eye
That it was clear as clear could be
I couldn't sell Tim for a fortune's fee.
I was shamed and sorry, I'll tell you plain,
And I took home Tim Tom Tay again.

LUCY LOVE'S SONG

I love a boy in Boulder,
I love a boy in Kew,
I love a boy in Bangalore
And one in Timbuktu.

I love a boy in Bari,
I love a boy in Rhyll,
I love a boy in Medicine Hat
And also in Seville.

I love a boy in Brooklyn,
I love a boy in Lille,
I love a boy in Alice Springs,
I love a boy in Kiel.

I love a boy in Ballarat,
I love a boy in Hayle,
I love a boy in Yellowknife,
I love a boy in Yale.

I love a boy in Buda,
I love a boy in Pest,
I love a boy in Trincomali,
I love a boy in Brest.

I love a boy in Brisbane,
I love a boy in Ayr,
I love a boy in Aldershot,
I love a boy in Clare.

I love a boy in Augusta
In the State of Maine,
But the boy I love the best of all
Lives just along the lane.

JILL AND JACK

Jill and Jack walked up the track
To find a pool of morning dew.
They took a pole, they took a pail,
Carried them both between the two.

Mani the Moon jumped low, jumped high,
Snatched them up into the sky.
Mani the Moon with fingers cold
Locked them in his house of gold.

When the moon is full and fair
You still may see them standing there,
And there they'll stay, I'm certain sure,
A thousand thousand years and more.

Pole and pail between the two:
Jill and Jack who walked the track
To find a pool of morning dew
And never came back. Poor Jill. Poor Jack.

Under the Hawthorn

Under the hawthorn
The white witch dwells
Who held in her noddle
A hundred spells,
But now she is old
As night and day,
Her memory gone
Quite far away
And try as she might
A spell to find
She can't call a single
One to mind.

She beats with her palm
The crown of her head,
She mumbles, she grumbles
From breakfast to bed,
She snaps her fingers,
She cracks her thumbs,
She whistles and whimpers,
She haws and hums,
But never a spell
Can she sing or say
Though you wait for a year,
A month and a day.

Her five wits once
Were winter-bright
As she moved on her mop-stick
Through the night
In her cloak of stars,
Her pointed hat,
And safe on her shoulder
Zal the cat,
But now she sits
As cold as a stone
Her flying days
All dead and done.

Her spells that were white
As the birch-tree wood
Are vanished away
And gone for good,
And still she scrapes
Her poor old brain
But there's none will tell her
It's all in vain
As she sits under
A failing sun.

Never a body.
Never a one.

A white witch was thought to practise only 'white' or bene-
ficial magic.

1, 2, 3, 4

1, 2, 3, 4,
Over the mountain,
Over the moor,
Here comes the soldier
Home from war.
    Tan, tan, tan.

4, 3, 2, 1,
Foul or fine,
Snow or sun,
Take it from me
It wasn't fun.

After the battle the Sergeant said,
'You've legs and arms
And you kept your head
And you're stony broke
But you're not stone dead.'

No more marching, no more drill,
I'm on my way
Down Homeward Hill
And I thank my stars
I'm breathing still.

'Take your pack, be on your way,'
I heard the Sergeant-
Major say,
'And live to fight
Another day.'
    Tan, tan, tan.

Sailors

Spider Webb,
Blanco White,
Pincher Martin,
Shiner Bright,

Doughy Baker,
Dolly Gray,
Smudger Smith,
Piggy May,

Tottie Bell,
Bunny Lake,
Stole a peck
Of Navy cake.[1]

[1] Navy cake was a rather heavy slab cake on sale in naval canteens.

Soapy Watson,
Dodger Green,
Pedlar Palmer,
Daisy Dean,

Snip Taylor,
Charley Peace,
Moggie Morgan,
Bodger Lees,

Dusty Miller,
Twisty Lane,
Made them bring it
Back again.

MRS BESSIE BUSYBODY

Mrs Bessie Busybody,
I declare,
Knows all the news
And some to spare.

From six in the morning
On the dot
Peers through the window
To see what's what.

Who's up early?
Who's up late?
Who wrote that
On the schoolyard gate?

Who's getting better?
Who's getting worse?
Who's had a visit
From the District Nurse?

Who turned the dust-bins
Upside down?
Who had a call
From P.C. Brown?

Who wasn't home
Till twelve last night?
Who broke his nose
In a fisticuff fight?

Who cracked the glass
In the garden frame?
Who didn't answer
When the rent-man came?

Who climbed the wall
At Number Five,
Took all the honey
Out of the hive,

Then as cool
As cool could be
Stole every apple
From the orchard tree?

Who let the bulldog
Off his chain?
Who had a case
Of best champagne?

Who's gone missing,
And who is due
To have a little baby
In a month or two?

Winter, spring-time,
Summer-time, fall,
Mrs Bessie Busybody
Knows it all.

DANDELION

Dandelion,
Yellow crown,
Now your petals
All are gone,
Speak to me
The time of day
As I blow
Your seeds away.

If at one breath
They are flown
I need never
Hurry home,
But if any
Seeds remain
I must to
My home again.

Dandelion,
Yellow head,
Tell me when
I shall be wed.
Country clock
Without a chime
When shall be
My wedding time?

Dandelion,
Tell me fair
How many children
I shall bear,
Or tell me true
As moon or sun
If there shall be
Never a one.

Dandelion,
Flowering clear
Through the seasons
Of the year
Teach me simple,
Teach me slow
All these things
That I must know.

LEONARDO

Leonardo, painter, taking
    Morning air
        On Market Street
Saw the wild birds in their cages
    Silent in
        The dust, the heat.

Took his purse from out his pocket
    Never questioning
        The fee,
Bore the cages to the green shade
    Of a hill-top
        Cypress tree.

'What you lost,' said Leonardo,
    'I now give to you
        Again,
Free as noon and night and morning,
    As the sunshine,
        As the rain.'

And he took them from their prisons,
    Held them to
        The air, the sky;
Pointed them to the bright heaven.
    'Fly!' said Leonardo.
        'Fly!'

This story is told of the Italian painter Leonardo da Vinci
(1452–1519).

LIE-ABED, LOAFER

Lie-abed, loafer, lazyboots, drone,
The hen-house is open,
The birds all flown.

Layabout, lounger, lubbard, poke,
The cows are eating acorns
Under the oak.

Idler, skiver, ne'er-do-well, doze,
The goat's in the wash-house
Swallowing the clothes.

Loller, lazylegs, clock-watcher, dream,
The cats are in the dairy
At the milk and cream.

Dawdler, do-little, lallygag, leech,
The sheep are a-stray
On the strong sea beach.

Scrimshanker, shirker, slumberer, slouch,
Wake up, rise up
From your couch:

Mammy and daddy are bound to be
Home from market
By half-past three.

DIGGORY PRANCE

Diggory Prance, Diggory Prance
Paid his bills with a bit of a dance.

He took a whistle, he took a drum,
He'd trip it and skip it till kingdom come.

He danced for the butcher who brought him meat
The whole of the length of Shambles Street.

He danced for the baker who baked his bread.
He danced for the tailor, his needle and thread.

He danced for his rent, he danced for his rates.
He danced for the builder who fixed his slates.

He danced for the cobbler who mended his shoe,
He danced for the plumber, the painter too.

He danced for his light, he danced for his heat.
He danced for his takeaway, sour-and-sweet.

He danced for the dentist, the doctor, the draper.
He danced for the price of his daily paper –

Till came a day when, 'Now, dear Diggory, please,
It's time,' said the Mayor, 'for this nonsense to
    cease.

'You must settle in cash and in coin what you owe
Or I fear I must ask you to pack up and go.'

But all of the people cried, 'What? What? What?
    What?
Send away Diggory? Certainly not!

'Send away Diggory? Never a chance!
We *like* to see Diggory doing a dance!

'We trust we are making it perfectly plain –
So please never mention the subject again.

'Never, whatever the wind or the weather,
Please never mention the subject again

'Of Diggory Prance, Diggory Prance
Who pays his bills with a bit of a dance.'

RAGGED, RAGGED ROBIN

Ragged, ragged robin
In the ditch and damp,
Light in the shade
Your red, red lamp;
Let it shine
Far and near,
Time for the cuckoo-
Call so clear.

Ragged, ragged robin
Glowing bright,
Fork-stem pointing
Left and right,
Tell the cuckoo
The month, the year;
Time the cuckoo
Was here, was here.

Ragged, ragged robin
Down by the splash,
Bring us the cuckoo
Grey as ash;
Bring us the cuckoo
Grey as slate,
Bring us the cuckoo
And bring his mate.

'Ragged robin' is a crimson flower whose real name is *Lychnis Flos-cuculi*. In Greek, *luchnos* means 'lamp' and *flos-cuculi* means 'flower of the cuckoo'.

JOHN TIDY

John Tidy's face is birthday-bright,
His hair is tight and trim,
His hands are scrubbed potato-white.
(It's not the same with Jim.)

John Tidy comes home cleaner than
When he went out to play,
And as for dirt and dust they seem
To fly the other way.

John Tidy likes to pass the time
By humming of a hymn
Or saying bits of poetry.
(It's not the same with Jim.)

All brushed and sweet from head to feet
John Tidy walks the town.
He's *never* seen on Castle Green
His shirt-tail hanging down.

John Tidy's good, John Tidy's gold
As any cherubim
(But as for Johnnie's brother, O,
It's not the same with him.)

If ever was a single pair
(The outside and the in)
As might be dock and daisy,
It's John, and Jim the twin.

Why I don't take to brother John
(So smart, so sleek, so slim)
I just can't put my finger on.
(It's not the same with Jim.)

ZOW-BUG

Zow-bug, zow-bug
Under the stone,
One of a hundred
Or one on your own,
Hurrying, flurrying
To and fro,
Fourteen legs
On the go, go, go,
Why are you hiding
Out of the light?
Waiting for day
To turn to night.

Zow-bug, zow-bug
Scurrying through
A world of dusk
And a world of dew,
Now that you've left
Your house of wood
Is it bad you are up to
Or is it good
Down in the garden
Dark and deep?
Taking a turn
Round the compost heap.

Zow-bug, zow-bug
By the long shore
Tell me who
You are waiting for:
Is it King Neptune,
A sole or a dab,
A Cornish pilchard
Or an ocean crab?
Who will you meet
On Newlyn Quay?
> *My great-great-grandaddy*
> *Lives in the sea.*

Zow-bug (sow-bug) is the country name for the woodlouse,
a land-living crustacean distantly related to the crab.

Dawn at Ballintoy

At Ballintoy, at Ballintoy
From dusk until the light of day
Upon the height an eye of white
Opens upon the moving bay.

And now it blinks, and now it winks,
That ships and sailors passing by
May know the ragged cliff that climbs
Between the waters and the sky.

A sea-bird hazards a first flight.
The sky burns blue, the sky burns free
As Ballintoy puts on the day
Beside the sounding of the sea.

TUESDAY MONDAY

Tuesday Monday
On a Sunday
Went to Saturday
For the one day;
Lost her way
At Hot Cross Friday
Found it again
By Thursday Highway.
Drove her car
But couldn't park it
Till she came
To Wednesday Market.
How to get home
After her fun day?
'Back to front,'
Said Tuesday Monday.

DON'T LET BABY

Don't let baby look in the mirror,
Don't let baby look in the glass
Lest its life be sad and sorry,
Lest its eyes go bent and boss.
Don't let baby look in the glass
Never until twelve months are past.

Cover up the glass with linen,
Turn it, turn it backsyvore.[1]
Don't let baby look in the mirror
Lest its life be wisht[2] and worried
Lest it fret and lest it roar
Half its days and then some more.

[1] backsyvore: back to front
[2] wisht: pale, wan

In earlier times it was believed to be unlucky for a baby to
see its reflection in a mirror or polished surface.

A LEAP OF LEOPARDS

A leap of leopards,
A sleuth of bears,
A clamour of rooks,
A husk of hares.

> *'Knawed that a'ready,' said Jacker.*
> *'No you never,' said Jan.*

A muster of peacocks,
A team of ducks,
A murder of crows,
A leash of bucks.

> *'Knawed that a'ready,' said Jacker.*
> *'No you never,' said Jan.*

A wing of plovers,
A sounder of swine,
A herd of curlews,
A drove of kine.

> *'Knawed that a'ready,' said Jacker.*
> *'No you never,' said Jan.*

A watch of nightingales,
A pod of seals,
A nye of pheasants,
A spring of teals.

     'Knawed that a'ready,' said Jacker.
     'No you never,' said Jan.

A chattering of choughs,
A bevy of quails,
A fall of woodcock,
A gam of whales.

     'Knawed that a'ready,' said Jacker.
     'No you never,' said Jan.

GIGLETS' MARKET

Tomorrow at Giglets' Market
I'll find a farmer who
Will take me as a hired man
For fifty weeks and two.

Tomorrow at Giglets' Market
I shall never be late
For I must go to market
To meet me with a mate.

I shall wear my Sunday suit,
My good cap on my head
And at my throat a handkerchief
Of yellow and of red.

In my right hand an oak stick
Ribboned with a bow,
And in my left I'll bear a pinch
Of holly and mistletoe.

I shall stand up straight and strong
And I shall never fear
To find a farmer who shall pay
Me ten gold pounds a year.

I'll stroll the setts and cobbles round,
I'll give the girls the eye
And with my besten Sunday boots
I'll make the sparks to fly.

And I shall meet a maid before
The ending of the day
And on the swings and roundabouts
We'll ride the hours away.

And when the fair is over
I'll ask her fresh and fine,
I'll ask her mammy, I'll ask her daddy
If I may call her mine.

She's certain sure to take me
And give to me her hand,
For I am a Cornish country boy
And I work the Cornish land.

When I was a boy in my home-town of Launceston, Giglets'
Market was held on the first Saturday after Christmas. It was
a hiring-fair, to which farm-workers (female as well as male)
came if they were seeking fresh employment. Traditionally it
was also the day when young men and women searched for
partners.

St Neot

St Neot, St Neot
I've heard tell
Spent his days
In a Holy Well.
Up to his neck
He was, was he,
With three little fish
For company.

St Neot sang
In water bright
The Book of Psalms
Morning to night
And then for supper
He would take
One little fish
To broil or bake.

When daylight came
St Neot would bring
Himself to swim,
Himself to sing
Where in the water
Pure and plain
Three little fish
They swam again.

The ninth-century St Neot, a famously small man, is believed to have lived in the Cornish village which bears his name. It is said that he had to stand on a stool when taking services so that the congregation could see him. Among the wonderful stained-glass windows in the church is one given by the young men of the parish in 1528, showing some of his adventures.

A Mermaid at Zennor

A mermaid at Zennor
Climbed out of the sea
By the seething Zennor shore.
Her gown was silver,
Her gown was gold
And a crown of pearl she wore,
She wore,
A crown of pearl she wore.

The Zennor bay
Burned peacock-blue,
White was the Zennor sand
Where she came up
By Zennor Head,
Comb in her crystal hand,
Her hand,
Comb in her crystal hand.

She stood before
The great church door
That open was and wide.
She gazed into
The mirror true
She carried at her side,
Her side,
She carried at her side.

Now Zennor men
Do love to sing
Their songs both great and small,
And Sampson Scown
The Squire's son
Sang sweetest of them all,
Them all,
Sang sweetest of them all.

The mermaid stepped
Out of the sun
And slowly entered in,
Her purpose fell
By charm or spell
Young Sampson for to win,
To win,
Young Sampson for to win.

And in a sea-deep
Tongue she sang
A song that none
Had known,
And choir and congregation stood
As they were made of stone,
Of stone,
As they were made of stone.

Only Young Sampson
Made reply
As clear as Cornish gold,
For he and only he
Could tell
The salt song that she told,
She told,
The salt song that she told.

She beckoned where
Young Sampson stood.
He took her by the hand.
And one and one
They walked them down
Towards the Zennor strand,
The strand,
Towards the Zennor strand.

And did they ever
Come again
There's never a one
Will own,
Where still in church
The people stand
As they were made of stone,
Of stone,
As they were made of stone.

Zennor is on the coast of the far west of Cornwall, and is a village once renowned for its singers. The church, dedicated to the virgin St Sinara or Sener, has a fifteenth-century bench-end bearing a splendid carving of its famous mermaid, complete with comb and glass.

HAZEL

Hazel fork
From hazel tree
Tell me where
The waters be.

Hazel shoot
In my hand
Bring me where
My true-love stands.

Hazel stem,
Hazel leaf,
Show me robber,
Show me thief.

Hazel twig,
Hazel bud,
Keep my house
From fire and flood.

Hazel stick,
Hazel wand,
Save me from
A water's end.

Hazel bush,
Hazel tree,
May you ever
Dwell by me.

There Once was a Man

There once was a man
Called Knocketty Ned
Who wore his cat
On top of his head.
Upstairs, downstairs,
The whole world knew
Wherever he went
The cat went too.

He wore it at work,
He wore it at play,
He wore it to town
On market day,
And for fear it should rain
Or the snowflakes fly
He carried a brolly
To keep it dry.

He never did fret
Nor fume because
He always knew
Just where it was.
'And when,' said Ned,
'In my bed I lie
There's no better nightcap
Money can buy.'

'There's no better bonnet
To be found,'
Said Knocketty Ned,
'The world around.
And furthermore
Was there ever a hat
As scared a mouse
Or scared a rat?'

Did ever you hear
Of a tale like that
As Knocketty Ned's
And the tale of his cat?

I WON'T GO HOME

I won't go home by the churchyard.
I know I'm sure to see
Wicked Willy Waters
Waiting there for me.

When there's never a light up in the sky
And the dark spreads like the sea
And the tawny owl goes *wick-e-wick*
In the dusky conker tree,

I know that Willy Waters,
Wrapped up in a big white sheet,
Is lying in wait by the churchyard gate
At the end of St Thomas Street.

He's fixed his face with whitewash,
His thumbs and fingers too,
And he'll shriek and he'll squall and he'll
        jump the wall
And cry out, 'Whoo-hoo-hoo!'

I won't mind ghosts or goblins
Or demons large or small.
They only live in story-books
And they're just not real at all,

And I know it's Willy Waters
Wrapped up in his silly sheet –
But why does he make my hair stand up
And my heart to skip a beat?

I won't go home by the churchyard.
I know I'm sure to see
Wicked Willy Waters
Waiting there for me.

DON'T CRY, SALLY

Don't cry, Sally,
Don't cry, Sue,
Don't tell your mammy
You don't know what to do.

Though on your cheek
The tears run down,
Put on your dancing shoes,
Skip round the town.

Don't cry, Dinah,
Don't cry, Dee,
There's many another
Swims in the sea.

58

Bind up your hair,
Sing and play,
Tomorrow is another
Dancing day.

Don't cry, Amabel,
Don't cry, Ann,
Now you know who's
My fancy man.

They say he's a shuffling
Scamping one,
But I know he'll love me
Till the world is done.

Early in the morning
When the songbirds sing
You shall hear
The church bells ring.

It's goodbye pretty,
It's goodbye plain
You never shall see
My face again.

Let Us Walk to the
Williwaw Islands

'Let us walk to the Williwaw Islands,'
Said the porcupine-pig to the snoar.
'If we turn to the right by the Isle of Wight
We'll be there by a quarter to four.'

'Never once have I gazed on the ocean,'
Said the snoar to the porcupine-pig.
'How I wish I could stray through its waters
     one day!
But isn't it awfully *big*?

'And I've heard that the waves of the briny
Are inclined to be salty and steep
Should one venture out more than ten yards
     from the shore –
And isn't it frightfully deep?'

'I can't think,' then replied his companion,
'Where you get such ideas, and that's flat.
A very old spoof who once sat on the roof
Told me something quite different from that.

'He remarked that the bright-bluey water
Stood quite still in the stiffest of breeze,
And the sea-salty waste had a sugary taste
And barely came up to one's knees.

'And he said that the Williwaw Islands
Are constructed of coconut cream
And Belgian chocs and peppermint rocks
And orange-and-lemonade streams.'

'I foresee both our lives very shortly
Becoming a terrible bore.
Time to get off the shelf! Find things
        out for oneself!'
Said the porcupine-pig to the snoar.

'On reflection, my dearest old crony,
I can do nothing more than agree.
Let us hurry away without further delay,'
Said the snoar to the porcupine-p.

So they packed up their goods and their chattels
(Whatever a chattel may be),
Some biscuits and bread and a buttery spread
And they hurried away to the sea.

But when, at the edge of the ocean,
They gazed at its foam and its fret,
Said the snoar, 'Gracious me, my friend
      porcupine-p.,
It's the frightfullest thing I've seen yet!'

For the water it tumbled and twisted
And jumped up right out of the bay,
And it just wasn't true that its colour was blue
But a horrible sort of a grey.

It wouldn't stand still for a moment.
It did nothing but surge and then swell.
It held a big ship in its watery grip
And it broke pieces off it as well.

Said the porcupine-pig, 'I've a feeling
As I gaze at the sea and the skies
That to walk all those miles to the Williwaw Isles
Might turn out to be rather unwise.'

And the snoar, who was sensibly smiling,
He lifted a sensible thumb,
And they turned in their track and they made
        their way back
The very same way they had come.

'We don't care for candy,' they chanted.
'Nor for sweets nor for treats large or small,
But if there's a spoof resting up on your roof
We'd be glad if you gave us a call, that's all.
We'd be glad if you gave us a call.'

I Saw a Saw-doctor

I saw a saw-doctor
Down by the saw-mill.
He said, 'I shall stay here,
Young fellow, until
With the aid of this saw-fly,
This rod and this line,
I catch me a saw-fish
On which I might dine.'

'Come sit on this saw-grass,'
The saw-doctor said,
'And hear the saw-sharpener
Cry overhead.'
But before I could join him,
Could speak or could say,
He sprang on his saw-horse
And galloped away.

The saw-sharpener is the country name for the great titmouse,
with its metallic two-noted call in spring.

HERE COMES TOM CLEVER

Here comes Tom Clever,
Best scholar ever.
> *Don't care, said Jim.*

Here comes Sally Heard,
Sings sweet as a bird.
> *Don't care, said Jim.*

Here comes Ned Hales,
Makes up tunes and tales.
> *Don't care, said Jim.*

Here comes Polly Friend,
Dived off Land's End.
> *Don't care, said Jim.*

Here comes Tony Stone,
Carves wood, carves bone.
       Don't care, said Jim.

Here comes Dolly Bray,
Swam Widemouth[1] Bay.
       Don't care, said Jim.

      Here comes Jack Fenner,
      Caught the Mermaid of Zennor.
            Don't care, said Jim.

      Here comes Jane Stead,
      Does sums in her head.
            Don't care, said Jim.

[1] pronounced Widmuth

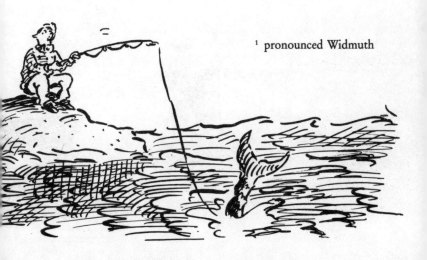

Here comes Zacky Sharp,
Plays the Jew's harp.
        Don't care, said Jim.

Here comes Johnnie Fine,
Sank Polmear Mine.
        Don't care, said Jim.

                Here comes Tamsin Fleet,
                Cooks a fine treat.
                        Don't care, said Jim.

                Here comes Daisy Fife,
                Make a good wife.
                        Going home, said Jim.

I WANT TO BE MONDAY

'I want to be Monday,' said Friday.
'It's such a dull spot that I've got.
I'd much rather have it than my day
That comes almost last of the lot.'

'What nonsense!' said Tuesday to Thursday.
'I don't think she knows what she's at.
There's no telling which is the worst day
Or which is the best, come to that.'

And Wednesday whispered to Sunday,
'I hope Monday doesn't say yes.
I've a feeling by changing the one day
We'll get in a terrible mess.'

Said Monday to Friday, 'A poor day?
But there's no one of whom we could speak
Who don't thank the stars that it's your day
At the end of a workaday week.'

'Of all the seven days,' declared Friday,
'I never thought I was the star!
If it's really that happy and high a day
I think I'll leave things as they are.
Yes, I think I'll leave things as they are.'

HERE WE GO ROUND THE
ROUND HOUSE

Here we go round the Round House
In the month of one,
Looking to the eastward
For the springing sun.
The sky is made of ashes,
The trees are made of bone,
And all the water in the well
Is stubborn as a stone.

Here we go round the Round House
In the month of two,
Waiting for the weather
To thaw my dancing shoe.
In St Thomas River
Hide the freckled trout,
But for dinner on Friday
I shall pull one out.

Here we go round the Round House
In the month of three,
Listening for the bumble
Of the humble-bee.
The light is growing longer,
The geese begin to lay,
The song-thrush in the church-yard
Charms the cold away.

Here we go round the Round House
In the month of four,
Watching a couple dressed in green
Dancing through the door.
One wears a wreath of myrtle,
Another, buds of thorn:
God grant that all men's children
Be as sweetly born.

Here we go round the Round House
In the month of five,
Waiting for the summer
To tell us we're alive.
All round the country
The warm seas flow,
The devil's on an ice-cap
Melting with the snow.

Here we go round the Round House
In the month of six;
High in the tower
The town clock ticks.
Hear the black quarter-jacks
Beat the noon bell;
They say the day is half away
And the year as well.

Here we go round the Round House
In the month of seven,
The river running thirsty
From Cornwall to Devon.
The sun is on the hedgerow,
The cattle in the stream,
And one will give us strawberries
And one will give us cream.

Here we go round the Round House
In the month of eight,
Hoping that for harvest
We shall never wait.
Slyly the sunshine
Butters up the bread
To bear us through the winter
When the light is dead.

Here we go round the Round House
In the month of nine,
Watching the orchard apple
Turning into wine.
The day after tomorrow
I'll take one from the tree
And pray the worm will do no harm
If it comes close to me.

Here we go round the Round House
In the month of ten,
While the cattle winter
In the farmer's pen.
Thick the leaves are lying
On the coppice floor;
Such a coat against the cold
Never a body wore.

Here we go round the Round House
In the month of eleven,
The sea-birds swiftly flying
To the coast of heaven.
The plough is in the furrow,
The boat is on the strand;
May I be fed on fish and bread
While water lies on land.

Here we go round the Round House
In the month of twelve,
The hedgers break the brier
And the ditchers delve.
As we go round the Round House
May the moon and sun
Guide us to tomorrow
And the month of one:
And life be never done.

The Round House, c.1830, is built over a broken market cross
at Launceston, in Cornwall.

Mrs Colón

Mrs Colón,
Christopher's gone
Sailing a boat
On the herring pond.

Says he's sure
That he knows best,
Steering, speering
West and west.

We gave him a call,
We gave him a shout
But he simply refuses
To turn about.

Will he remember
To keep in his head
The sooth of what
The schoolmaster said,

That the world is flat
With never a bend,
Go too far
And you're off the end?

Mrs Colón,
What's to be done?
Christopher's sailing
The herring pond.

In English-speaking countries the Italian sailor Cristoforo
Colombo (or, in Spain, Cristóbal Colón) is known as Christopher Columbus.

PRINCE IVO

Prince Ivo by the castle stood
He built with his own hand.
He looked towards the wandering sea,
He looked towards the land.

Tall was the yellow tower where
Prince Ivo's flag was flown.
The moat was wide, the moat was deep,
The gate was all of stone.

'And none there is,' Prince Ivo said,
'Shall bring my castle low,
For I am Lord of all I see
Wherever I may go.'

But there was one that heard him speak
And by his castle lay
Crept up the evening strand and washed
His house of sand away.

And when at sunfall Ivo came
Down to the silent shore
There was no sign of wall or tower.
His castle was no more.

Never a sign did Ivo show
Of sorrow or of pain,
But took his sturdy spade in hand
To build his house again.

Prince Ivo smiled and shook his head.
Softly I heard him say,
'Tomorrow, but tomorrow
Is another day.'

LION

That's Saint Jerome, my master, over there
Writing a book in Latin. All of five
Years he's been at it. The two of us share
A lodging in this shabby desert cave.

Most folk find him a bit cantankerous.
Tongue like a knife. Gets in an awful tear
With scholars, pilgrims, seeking his advice
And (worst of all) tourists who come to stare.

But here I must make one thing very plain:
This wise man has a heart as well as head.
Long years ago he eased a giant thorn
Out of my paw, while other people fled.

He watched, he tended me, quite unafraid,
Till once again I could both race and run,
And then it was a serious vow I made:
I would protect him till my life was done.

I've surely got my work cut out. But then,
I sleep with open eyes, as you will see
In paintings of us by quite famous men,
Although at first you may not notice me.

Sometimes he beats his breast with a flat stone.
Sometimes he gives a very little groan.
(I can't think why.) Well, be that as it may,
To all who call on him from near, from far:
Treat this great scholar with respect, I say.
                    Grrrrr!

St Jerome lived from about the year 342 to 420. He translated
most of the Bible from its original languages into Latin.

In medieval times the lion was thought to sleep with its eyes
open and so to be at all times watchful and alert.

81

My Name is Little Mosie

My name is Little Mosie,
I lie among the bushes,
My cradle is a sailing-boat
Of yellow reeds and rushes.

It was my sister brought me
Beside the swimming water.
One morning very early came
The King of Egypt's daughter.

She took me to her palace,
She laid me in her bed,
She dressed me in the finest shirt
Of gold and silver thread.

She put a circlet on my brow,
A ring upon my hand,
'And you shall be,' she said to me,
'A Prince of Egypt land.'

But now, in a far country,
I tend my field-flock well
And none there is to listen
To the mystery I tell:

When I was Little Mosie
I lay among the bushes
Cradled in a sailing-boat
Of yellow reeds and rushes.

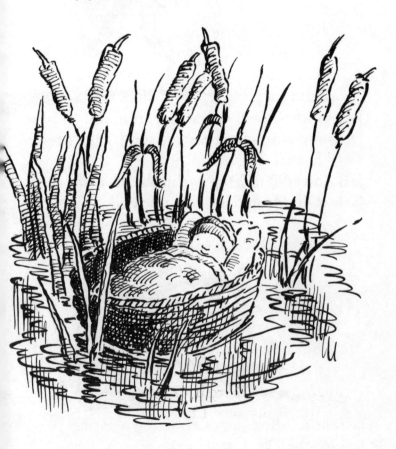

JACK

Jack-o'-the-Bowl[1] drinks the cream in the byre
Jack-in-the-Smoke turns the spit by the fire

Jack-in-the-Pulpit[2] grows in the deep wood
Jack-in-the-Irons[3] is up to no good

Jack-in-the-Box jumps about on a spring
Jack-o'-the-Clock makes the hour bell ring

Jack-in-the-Basket[4] stands in the sea-spray
Jack-o'-the Lantern will lead you astray

Jack-in-the-Green wears the leaves of a tree
Jack-in-the-Cellar's a baby to be

Jack-in-a-Bottle[5] fine feathers a nest
Jack-out-of-Office is taking a rest

Jack-at-a-Pinch gives a hand when he can
Jack-by-the-Hedge[6] stands up straight as a man

Jack-a-Dreams dozes all day in the sun
Jack-of-all-Trades is . . .

[1] house ghost or goblin   [2] North-American wild plant
[3] tall ghostly figure, frightens the traveller
[4] basket on a pole, indicating a sand-bank
[5] long-tailed titmouse, builds a bottle-shaped nest
[6] plant of the wallflower family, sometimes called garlic
mustard

TOMORROW IS SIMNEL SUNDAY

Tomorrow is Simnel Sunday
And homeward I shall steer
And I must bake a simnel cake
For my mother dear.

I'll fetch me almonds, cherries,
I'll fetch me pot and pan,
I'll fetch me salt, I'll fetch me spice,
I'll fetch me marzipan.

With milk and eggs and butter
And flour as fair as snow
And raisins sweet and candied treat
I'll set it all to go.

And I shall search for violets
That scent the homeward way
For tomorrow is Simnel Sunday
And it is Mothering Day.

Simnel (or Mothering) Sunday is the fourth Sunday in Lent.
Following an old custom, children visited their parents for the
day and took gifts of cake and flowers.

Who's That up There?

'Who's that up there?'
Called Jinny-lie-by-the-Church.

'Didn't hear a sound
All morning,'
Said Tom Snoring.

'Nor I,'
Said Little Jack Found.

'Seeming you're dreaming,'
Grizzled old Grannie Mutton.

'Children at play!'
Yawned Ben-sleep-till-Doomsday.

'Certainly so,'
Breathed Danny Button.

Said Jinny, 'Well,
I fancy I hear a bell
And Parson Hook
Mumbling out of his book,
And feet that do tread
The green overhead.'

'Think you're right,'
Muffled Granfer Blight.
'I'm sure as sure
Someone or other,
Middle of summer,
Is coming to make
One more.'

'Ain't enough room,'
Whispered Sally Coombe.
'Best they held steady.
Bit of a squash here
Already.'

'Hope it ain't Fiddler Niall,
Him with the teeth and the smile,'
Said Long Tommy Tile.

'Or Journeyman Seth,
Hedger and ditcher,
Him with the cider
On his breath,'
Said Peter the Preacher.

'Or that Mrs Handle,
Talks nothing but scandal,
Or young Peter Blunder
With the bull-chest and the voice
Like thunder,'
Said Bessie Boyce.

'Or Jessie Priddle the teacher
– Bossy old creature –
She'd soon tell us all
What to do,'
Said Barty Blue.

'O dear!' they sighed
With a groan.

'Why can't they leave us
Alone?'
Cried Crusty-the-Baker.
'It's peaceful and easeful
We are
In God's little acre.'

DANIEL GUMB

Daniel Gumb lived all alone
In a Cornish cave of granite stone,
Granite table and chair and bed,
Granite pillow to rest his head,
Granite roof and granite floor
And a sliding, gliding granite door
By Cheesewring Hill on Bodmin Moor.

He studied the stars and planets and then
(Hammer and chisel for a pen)
He chipped the drift of what he'd found
On bits of rock that lay around,
And over the moor the folk would come
For there wasn't a problem, wasn't a sum
As couldn't be solved by Daniel Gumb.

Daniel Gumb in the midst of life
Took to himself a loving wife.
She shared his crowst,[1] she shared his cell,
She gave him a gaggle of Gumbs as well
And he wrote on a stone for all to see:
'1735. D.G.'

Stranger, under Cheesewring Hill
In summer sun, in winter chill,
Search for the stone. It lies there still.

[1] crowst (a Cornish word): food

Famous in his day, the stone-cutter Daniel Gumb was known
as 'The Mountain Philosopher'. He died in 1776 and is buried
in the parish of Linkinhorne.

SAWSON SLY

Sawson Sly
Open your eye,
Here's a maid says
You married her
Last July,
Promised a cottage
Of slate and stone
Your grannie had given you
For your own,
An orchard of seven
Apple trees,
A lop-eared pig
And a hive of bees,
Five milch-cows,
A field of hay
And a pony and trap
For market day;
Swears the Parson
Made you a pair
Twelve of the clock
At Calstock Fair.

She's come with her daddy,
She's come with her mam
And a dear little darling
In a pram,
And just beyond
The garden gate
Her ten tall brothers
Stand and wait.
She's a shiny ring
As once was yours
And says you turned her
Out of doors
With never a coat,
A bonnet or cap.
Sawson, what do you say
To that?

Sawson Sly
Open your eye,
Here's a maid says
You married her
Last July.

CLIMB THE STAIR

Climb the stair, Katie,
Climb the stair, Paul,
The sun is down
On the orchard wall.

All through the valley
The air turns blue,
Silvers the meadow-grass
With dew.

High in the tower
The scritch owl cries,
Watching where darkest
Darkness lies.

The bats round the barnyard
Skim and stray
From last of light
To first of day.

Unseen, the water
Winds on the weir,
Sings a night-song
For all to hear.

Good night, Katie,
Good night, Paul,
Sleep till the new day
Comes to call.

INDEX OF FIRST LINES